EVERGLADES FOREVER

RESTORING AMERICA'S GREAT WETLAND

BY **TRISH MARX** ✦ PHOTOGRAPHS BY **CINDY KARP**

LEE & LOW BOOKS INC. ✦ NEW YORK

For Molly, with love — T.M.

For my nephew, Alexander — C.K.

Text copyright © 2004 by Trish Marx
Photographs copyright © 2004 by Cindy Karp

LEE & LOW BOOKS Inc., 95 Madison Avenue, New York, NY 10016
leeandlow.com

Many thanks to Dr. Grace Nebb, Principal, Jacquelyn (Jackie) Stone, teacher, and the children in her 2003–2004 fifth-grade class, and Regina Frances, counselor, Avocado Elementary School, Homestead, Florida; Eric Chong, Robert's father; Mindy McNichols, Esq., Miami-Dade County Board of Education; Buffalo Tiger's Airboat Tours; Shannon Mayorga, Audubon of Florida; Curtis Morgan, *The Miami Herald;* Dr. Joel Trexler, Department of Biological Sciences, Florida International University; Randy Smith, South Florida Water Management District; Sandy Dayhoff, Outreach Educational Specialist, Ranger Ben Niedbalski, Ranger Jim Lovelace, and Ranger John McKinney, Everglades National Park; and Doug Vogel.

And special thanks to Dr. Maria del Rio Rumbaites, Hugo Mesenbring, and Ana Maria Mesenbring.

Manufactured in China

Book design by Tania Garcia
Book production by The Kids at Our House

The text is set in Bembo

(HC) 10 9 8 7 6 5 4 3 2
(PB) 10 9 8 7 6 5 4 3 2 1
First Edition

Library of Congress Cataloging-in-Publication Data
Marx, Trish.
    Everglades forever: restoring America's great wetland / by Trish Marx ; photographs by Cindy Karp.— 1st ed.
        p. cm.
    ISBN 978-1-58430-164-6 (hc)
    ISBN 978-1-60060-339-6 (pb)
    1. Natural history—Florida—Everglades—Juvenile literature. I. Karp, Cindy, ill. II. Title.
QH105.F6M274 2004
508.759'39—dc22   2004002934

FRONT COVER: *Double Crested Cormorant overlooking the Everglades*
BACK COVER: *Ms. Stone and her fifth-grade class*
TITLE PAGE: *Boat ride through sawgrass prairie*

RIGHT: *Everglades National Park*

"Where the grass and the water are,

there is the heart,

the current,

the meaning

of the Everglades."

Marjory Stoneman Douglas, 1890–1998
Everglades activist, environmentalist, author

Double Crested Cormorant overlooking the Everglades

AVOCADO ELEMENTARY SCHOOL

"In the whole world, there is only one Everglades," Ms. Stone told her fifth-grade class at Avocado Elementary School.

The Everglades is a wide, shallow, slow-moving river that spreads like a sheet over southern Florida. As the water makes its way to the ocean, it forms a wetland wilderness of prairies and sloughs, tree islands and pine forests, dense stands of cypress trees and brackish ocean inlets. This barely moving water is the life force of the Everglades, and most of it comes in the form of rain that falls during the wet season. Each wet and dry season renews the cycle and mix of plant and animal life that is special to the Everglades.

Ms. Stone's class was studying the Everglades because they live in Homestead, Florida, a town perched on the eastern edge of this unique natural environment. The plants, animals, water, and weather of the Everglades form an ecosystem, a community that supports life, found nowhere else on Earth. In recognition of the special significance it holds in the world, Everglades National Park has been designated an International Biosphere Reserve, a World Heritage Site, and a Wetland of International Importance.

"The Everglades is in danger," Ms. Stone continued, "and it has been for many years." Today the Everglades is only half as big as it was one hundred years ago. Much of the land has been drained of water and used to develop farms and towns, and some of the water is polluted with chemicals and other substances from this development. All this changes the kinds of plants and animals that can live in the Everglades.

Ms. Stone opened a book of paintings by the famous naturalist John James Audubon. In the early 1800s, Audubon painted many of the birds in the Everglades. He said the sky used to be dark for minutes at a time with the flocks flying overhead.

The children looked out the window. It was hard to imagine that many birds. The Everglades now has only one tenth the number of birds it had two hundred years ago, and some species are endangered. In 1947 part of the Everglades became a national park to protect endangered birds and the thousands of other kinds of animals and plants that live there. Now that part is in serious danger too, because the amount, makeup, and distribution of water flowing into it from other parts of Florida have changed.

Ms. Stone showed the class a large map of southern Florida, including the part of the ocean called Florida Bay.

"This is Everglades National Park," Ms. Stone said, indicating the tip of Florida. She also pointed out a large lake, Lake Okeechobee. The Everglades began thousands of years ago in the Kissimmee River Basin, just north of Lake Okeechobee. The water flowed from the basin into the lake and then started a long, slow journey to the ocean. But in the last one hundred years, that journey has been interrupted.

What happened? the class wanted to know. Why have there been so many changes in the Everglades?

Ms. Stone and her students decided that a few of the children might visit the Everglades, find out more about these changes, and then report back to the class. This would help the students better understand the Everglades and prepare for their field trip to the national park that was coming up in a few weeks.

Four students—Tiler, Conrado, Robert, and Vedantee—volunteered to visit the Everglades. Robert's dad agreed to take them on a weekend trip. They planned to go to the northern part of Everglades National Park and the Miccosukee Reservation, which is located at the boundary of the park.

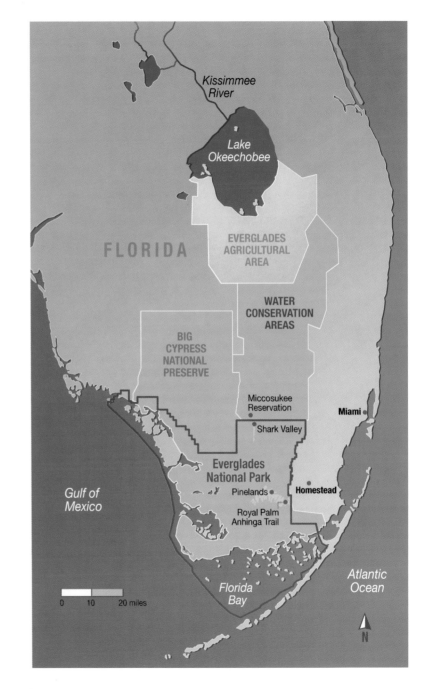

SHARK VALLEY

The first place Conrado, Vedantee, Robert, and Tiler visited was Shark Valley in Shark River Slough, an eight-mile-wide area of soft marshy ground and slowly moving water. The slough used to be twenty-five miles wide, but drainage and development have reduced it to one third its original size. The freshwater in the slough flows south to the Shark River and then to Florida Bay. When the freshwater mixes with the salt water of the ocean, it becomes brackish, or partly salty.

A park ranger named Ben rode up on his bicycle and greeted the children. Rangers often take time from their job of watching over the environment to educate visitors about the park.

"We're here to find out why the Everglades is in danger," said Conrado.

"And why it's so special too," added Tiler.

"You've come to the right place," said Ranger Ben. "Follow me. I'm going to take you on a tram ride into Shark Valley."

The children jumped on the tram. Everywhere they looked they saw water and grass. Ranger Ben told them another name for the Everglades is "River of Grass" because even if you can't see the water moving, you can always see the endless grass that grows out of the river and bends in the wind, pointing in the direction of the ocean. Marjory Stoneman Douglas gave the Everglades this name. She was one of the first people who worked to protect and restore the Everglades. She moved to Florida as a young woman in 1915 and fell in love with the Everglades. Douglas spent so much

ABOVE: *River of Grass*

of her life working to save the Everglades that she became known as the "Mother of the 'Glades."

The sloughs in Shark Valley are about three feet deep, with limestone bottoms formed by seashells left thousands of years ago. Growing out of the muck that covers the limestone is sawgrass, a special kind of grasslike vegetation.

"Here, feel this," Ranger Ben said, holding out a piece of sawgrass.

"Ouch," said Vedantee. "It's sharp."

"Sawgrass is so sharp that when explorers in the Everglades many years ago got lost, their clothes were cut to rags by the teethlike edges of the grass," explained Ranger Ben.

Sawgrass helps keep the Everglades healthy by filtering the water, but the main filters of Everglades water are spongy, slimy algae called periphyton. Periphyton are also the base of the Everglades food

web. Small water-dwelling invertebrates such as insects, snails, and shrimp eat the periphyton; other small animals such as crayfish, fish, turtles, and snakes eat the invertebrates; larger fish and wading birds such as egrets eat the small animals; and finally alligators and raccoons eat the larger fish and birds.

LEFT: *Periphyton*

ABOVE: *Great Egret*

RIGHT: *Alligator*

Ahead, two Great Blue Herons blocked the tramway, each holding its wings out to a full six feet. Instead of fighting for a feeding spot, herons display with their wings and dance, to show their strength, until one backs down. An alligator lay motionless in a water-filled hole it had dug, full from its last meal. Two deer stepped quietly through the sawgrass.

Soon the tram stopped, and everyone got off to climb an observation tower that rose high above the Everglades. Vedantee, Conrado, Tiler, and Robert ran to the top. The sky was endless. They could see for miles and miles. Small tree islands called hammocks rose a few inches above the water. Deer and Florida panthers live on these patches of dry land, hidden in the cover of the trees. This is what much of the Everglades looked like for thousands of years.

12   ABOVE: *Deer in sawgrass*   RIGHT: *Overlooking the Everglades*

MICCOSUKEE RESERVATION

After leaving Shark Valley, Robert, Tiler, Vedantee, and Conrado visited the Miccosukee Reservation, located on the northern boundary of Everglades National Park. In 1830 the United States government adopted the Indian Removal Act, which required that all Indians in the southeastern part of the country be relocated to the west. To escape going to Oklahoma Territory, the Miccosukees fled to the densest part of the Everglades and hid there. Today their descendants still live in this area.

On the reservation, the children went on an airboat ride through the sawgrass prairie. Ernie, the captain of the boat, was their guide through this part of the Everglades. He told them the Miccosukees call the Everglades *Pa-hay-okee,* or "Grassy River." Then he said he would help the children see things about the Everglades the way the Miccosukees do.

Ernie turned the boat down a canal and into the vast prairie of water, sawgrass, and low trees. The children peered over the side of the boat as it edged toward a floating mass of vegetation. Resting on top was an alligator. Spikes on the alligator's back act like solar panels, soaking up warmth and energy from the sun.

Next the boat entered a narrow clearing where Conrado, Vedantee, Robert, and Tiler saw a hammock. The grassy patch of land was mostly hidden in the sawgrass. Surrounding the grass were hardwood trees, their branches tangled together as if they were guarding the island. The Miccosukees lived on hammocks until the 1940s. The trees acted as a natural air-conditioning system, providing protection from the heat of the

Alligator absorbing energy from the sun

sun. The Miccosukees grew crops on other hammocks nearby. Wooden racks were used to dry sweet potatoes, corn, and other vegetables. Today many Miccosukees live in modern homes in a village they built on Miccosukee land in the Everglades or in other parts of the Everglades, but some still practice the traditional way of life, living on hammocks.

16

ABOVE: *Wooden racks for drying vegetables*   RIGHT: *Harvesting sugarcane in south Florida*

The Miccosukees believe that everything goes around the Earth in the circle of life. All plant and animal and human life is connected, and it is important to respect all forms of life and live within the natural life cycles of the Everglades. When large numbers of settlers started moving to Florida in the 1920s, they looked at the abundant sunshine and ample rainfall and thought the land would be good for crops. They built canals to drain large parts of the Everglades water and used the land for farms and homes. The canals interrupted the water and kept it from flowing naturally over the land. The settlers also built levees and dikes to hold back the water. The canals, levees, and dikes allowed the settlers to control and save the water so it could be used for washing, drinking, irrigation, and factory production. This meant there was less water for the plants and animals of the Everglades.

As the airboat moved on, the children studied the tangle of plants floating in the water. What Tiler, Conrado, Robert, and Vedantee couldn't see in the water was the pollution that was the result of farming and industrial development. One of the substances harming the Everglades is phosphorus, which comes mostly from fertilizers used on farm crops. Because Everglades water is naturally very low in phosphorus, any rise in the level of this natural element can damage the environment. Plants, such as sawgrass, that grow best in water low in phosphorus, are pushed out by other plants, especially cattails. The cattails choke out the sawgrass and the animals that depend on the sawgrass for food and shelter.

The Miccosukees felt that this draining and polluting of water were destroying the natural Everglades life cycles and disrupting the circle of life that renewed all living things on Earth.

Did the Miccosukees do something to help the Everglades? the children wanted to know. Did they try to change the quality of the water, or the way it flowed, so the circle of life could continue?

LEFT: *Cattails*   ABOVE: *Rerouting Everglades water*

In 1993 the Miccosukees joined environmental agencies, interest groups such as farmers and ranchers, and concerned citizens in their lawsuits against the state of Florida over how the state was enforcing the federal Clean Water Act of 1972. They said the water flowing into the Everglades contained higher levels of pollution than allowed by the Clean Water Act. As a result, a new law—the Everglades Forever Act—was passed by the Florida legislature in 1994. This law provided funding for plans to help reduce levels of phosphorus and pollutants in the water.

One way pollution is controlled under the Everglades Forever Act is through the use of huge artificial marshes to clean the water before it flows to the Everglades. Giant pumps force the water into the marshes where plants, such as prairie grass and periphyton, soak up phosphorus and other damaging chemicals and pollutants. It can take as long as six months for polluted farm water to flow through an artificial marsh and make its way, significantly cleaner, into the Everglades.

The marshes help improve the quality of the Everglades water, but the problem of how much water is left for the plants and animals of the Everglades remains. To make sure there will be enough water for the Everglades and all the people, farms, and industrial uses in the area, a plan to restore the Everglades was developed. In 2000 the state of Florida, a federal government agency called the Army Corps of Engineers, and various environmental agencies, Indian tribes, and farmers proposed a blueprint, a detailed outline, of how to restore the Everglades ecosystem and make sure the water is used wisely. This developed into the Comprehensive Everglades Restoration Plan consisting of more than sixty separate projects. The restoration will take at least thirty years to complete and cost billions of dollars. The United

Clearing sugarcane field for construction of marsh to clean Everglades water

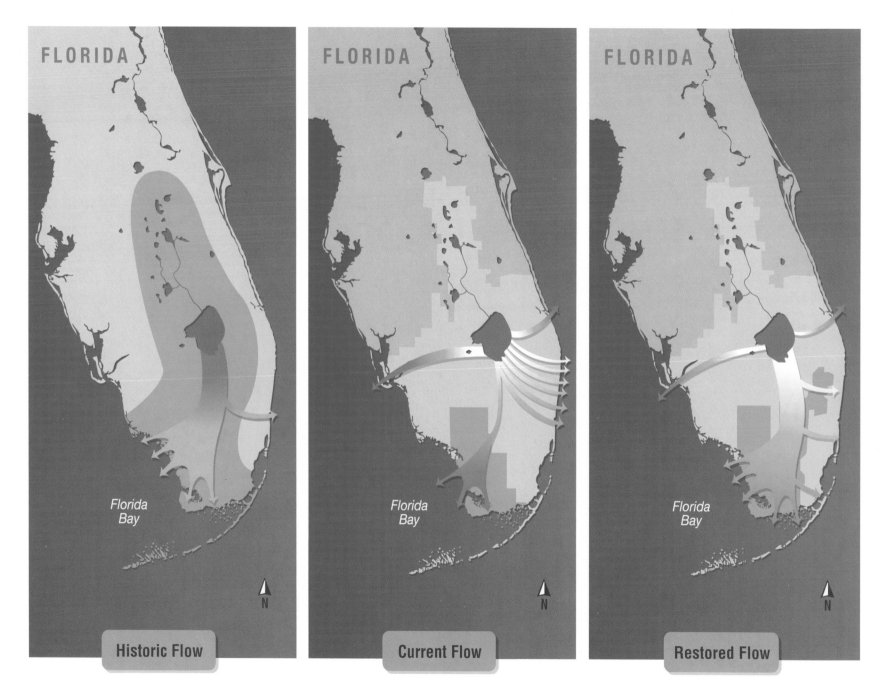

FLORIDA

Florida
Bay

Historic Flow

FLORIDA

Florida
Bay

Current Flow

FLORIDA

Florida
Bay

Restored Flow

Projects to recapture and redirect water flowing through the Everglades are part of the Everglades Restoration Plan

States Congress agreed to support the plan. The state of Florida and the federal government will share the cost. Such a large-scale restoration of a natural system has never before been attempted.

Some of the projects will help manage the water in the Everglades by storing it during the rainy season in huge underground aquifers, which are natural storage tanks that have formed in rock deep in the Earth. The aquifers will be reinforced and fitted with pumps, and the water will be pumped to various parts of the Everglades when water levels get too low. If these projects work, all the habitats of the Everglades, such as the sawgrass prairies and the hardwood hammocks, will get the water they need, and the plants and animals that have adapted to each habitat will be able to continue finding food and reproducing.

Other projects call for the removal of roads, canals, levees, and dikes in the Everglades to restore some of the natural flow of water. Originally, when water flowed like a shallow, slow-moving, uninterrupted sheet over southern Florida, some of it sank through the porous limestone bottom and kept the underground aquifers filled with freshwater. Some water flowed into the wetlands that served as nurseries for new life. And some water evaporated and helped create the rain that supported all life in the Everglades. Restoring a portion of the original water flow will help ensure the survival of these important parts of the Everglades ecosystem.

As the children ended their boat ride and their visit to the Everglades, they realized how lucky they were to have such a unique natural environment close to their homes and school. They also realized they could share responsibility for the future of the Everglades as they grew into adults. They could help protect this wild and wonderful place, just like all the people they had met on their trip.

AVOCADO ELEMENTARY SCHOOL

Back at Avocado School, Tiler, Vedantee, Robert, and Conrado reported to the class about their trip to the Everglades. They described Shark Valley and the Miccosukee Reservation and told about the slough, sawgrass, and hammock habitats they visited and the plants and animals they saw. They explained the effects of pollution, and how draining the Everglades for farms and towns was changing it forever. Then they explained how the Miccosukees, state and national governments, and environmental groups are working hard to restore what is left of the Everglades ecosystem.

"It's a *big* plan," said Conrado.

"It's going to cost *billions* of dollars!" exclaimed Vedantee.

"And it's going to take at least thirty years," added Tiler.

"So when we get older, *we* will be making decisions about the Everglades," said Robert.

"That's right," said Ms. Stone. "So it's important that we find out as much as we can about the Everglades. When we go on our field trip next week, we'll learn more about sawgrass prairies, sloughs, and hammocks. We'll also learn about two other habitats—mangrove swamps and the Pinelands—and visit a very special part of the sawgrass prairie."

"We simply cannot let everything be destroyed. We can't do that, not if we want water. We've got to take care of what we have."

Marjory Stoneman Douglas

Overlooking sawgrass on Anhinga Trail

ROYAL PALM
AND THE PINELANDS

On the morning of the field trip, the bus traveled west from Avocado School. The children saw the landscape change from houses and shopping centers to a flat, grassy prairie that met the horizon miles away. Soon they arrived at the Royal Palm Visitor Center, part of Everglades National Park.

Ms. Stone had arranged for the class to meet Ranger Jim at the visitor center. From there the ranger led them to the start of the Anhinga Trail, a boardwalk circling into a slough. It was the dry season, which lasts from December through April, so the water levels were low. But there is a deep part of the slough at the beginning of the trail that never dries up. Around the edge of this part, large waterbirds called Anhingas sunned their wings. Anhingas hold out their wings to thermoregulate, or regulate their body temperature, by soaking up the sun's energy to keep their bodies warm. An Osprey, a fish-eating hawk, waited in a tree for a flash of fish in the water. In the distance an egret stood in the sawgrass, and a flock of endangered wood storks flew overhead.

"Right now you'll see many animals close together around the deeper water areas," said Ranger Jim. Fish and smaller water animals had migrated to these deep water areas to search for food. Wading birds, alligators, Ospreys, and Cormorants (large diving birds with bright green eyes) followed to feed on the fish and smaller animals. Alligators also use their tails, snouts, and feet to dig deep holes, which fill with water. These holes are places for alligators to cool off while they wait for a meal of the small animals that are attracted to the water-filled holes. During the wet season, which lasts from May through November, water covers much of the land. Then the animals spread out because the water that carries their food is spread out.

The Everglades has wet and dry seasons, but it also has wetter and drier areas caused by how high the land is above the water level. Even a few inches of elevation can make a difference in how wet or

ABOVE: *Great Blue Heron feeding on fish*   RIGHT: *Mangrove trees*

dry the soil remains throughout the year. These differences in moisture help create unique habitats, each with its own special set of plants and animals.

One of the lowest Everglades habitats is the mangrove swamp, which is named for the mangrove trees that line the islands and bays leading into the ocean. Fresh rainwater flows toward these areas and mixes with the salty ocean water, making the water in mangrove swamps brackish. The mangrove trees have specially adapted roots and leaves so they can live in this salty, muddy water. The swamps also serve as nurseries for shrimp, bonefish, and other marine animals that need a protected place to grow before they head to the ocean. If the brackish water in mangrove swamps changes, these animals

cannot survive. Since two goals of the Restoration Plan are to allow Everglades water to flow more naturally to the ocean and to regulate the amount of freshwater flowing during each season, animals of the mangrove swamps—including pelicans, sea turtles, and the endangered American crocodiles and manatees—will be helped to survive.

The class was too far from the ocean to see a mangrove swamp, but as they walked the Anhinga Trail, the children saw several of the habitats Tiler, Conrado, Robert, and Vedantee had told them about. The slough filled with slow-moving water stretched in the distance. A sawgrass prairie covered the shallow parts of the slough, and in the distance the rounded domes of hardwood hammocks rose above the surface of the water.

As the children came to the end of the Anhinga Trail, Ranger Jim pointed out a gumbo limbo tree. "It's also called a tourist tree," he said, "because the bark of the tree peels off, just like the skin of sunburned tourists." Then he directed the children back to the bus for a short ride to a pine forest called the Pinelands.

Ranger Jim took the class on a hike through the Pinelands, one of the driest habitats in the Everglades. The sunlight filtered through the trees. Everything was quieter than on the Anhinga Trail. The floor of the Pinelands is covered with cabbage palms, marlberry bushes, blue porter flowers, and other vegetation that help absorb sounds from the outside world.

"This is where you'll find solution holes," Ms. Stone told the children. They searched the forest for the large holes that have been carved out of the limestone by tannic acid, a chemical formed when rainwater mixes with the pine needles and other leaves in the forest. Small animals live, feed, and raise their young in the solution holes. The children also watched as a tiny yellow tree snail nestled under the bark of a tree, eating a growth on the tree called lichen. They saw a Red-Shouldered Hawk swirl in the sky, and they waited for a golden orb spider to catch its next meal in its web close to the ground.

Hiking through the Pinelands

As they walked through the Pinelands, the children talked with Ms. Stone and Ranger Jim about the circle of life—the Miccosukee belief that all plant and animal and human life is connected. They had seen this today in the habitats they visited. The children also realized how terrible it would be if the habitats in this part of the Everglades were not protected from the effects of farming and development that were still putting the Everglades in danger. What would happen to all the unique plants and animals they had seen? Ranger Jim said they could help by conserving water, even when brushing their teeth or washing their faces, because most of the water used in southern Florida comes from the Everglades. With responsible water conservation, the Everglades Restoration Plan could, over the next thirty years, restore a healthy balance so all living things—plants, animals, and people—will be able to live side by side in the only *Pa-hay-okee,* "Grassy River," in the world.

It was the end of a long day for the class, but there was one more part of the Everglades to visit. Ms. Stone and Ranger Jim led the children into an open space hidden at the end of the hiking trail.

"This is a finger glade," Ms. Stone said. "It's a small part of the sawgrass prairie that does not stay wet all year." During the wet season, the finger glade would be filled with water and fish. But now the ground, which is higher than the larger sawgrass prairies, was dry and hard.

"For a few minutes you can walk as far as you like and enjoy the finger glade," said Ms. Stone.

The children fanned out. Some pretended they were birds, flying low overhead. Others studied the sawgrass, pretending to be explorers discovering the glade. Still others talked about how the hard ground on which they were walking would turn into a lake deep enough for fish to swim through during the wet season. And some just lay on their backs, looking at the sky and the ring of trees around the glade.

When the children came back, they sat in a circle close to Ms. Stone.

"Close your eyes," said Ms. Stone, "and listen."

"Do you hear cars?" she whispered.

"Do you hear sirens?"

"Do you hear people?"

"What do you hear?"

Silence.

"You are not going to find silence like this anyplace else in the world," Ms. Stone said quietly.

"This glade is protected by a circle of trees and marshes and natural wildlife. It is far from the noise of the outside world. It's full of *silence.* Any time you are in a sawgrass prairie like this one, stop and listen to the silence."

The sun was setting over the Everglades as the class walked back to the bus. Birds flew low over the sawgrass prairie. It was a peaceful time, a time for everything to settle down for the night. The children knew that for the near future the Everglades would

look the same, and might even be almost the same. They also knew about the dangers facing the Everglades, and that it would not stay the same unless people watched over it and took care of it.

Restoring the Everglades will take a long time, and it may never be finished. But the children knew they could play a part as they grew older. They had learned that they too were a part of the Everglades, connected in the same circle of life with the tiniest insect and largest alligator. They knew that someday in the not-too-distant future, responsibility for the Everglades would pass on to them. They would become the guardians and protectors of the only Everglades in the world, helping this wild and wonderful place go on *forever*.

"Perhaps even in this last hour . . . the vast, magnificent, subtle and unique region of the Everglades may not be utterly lost."

Marjory Stoneman Douglas

Flock of White Ibis

AUTHOR'S NOTE

Cindy Karp lives in Florida and has spent many days in the Everglades. I had been there only once, years ago, but I remember being moved by the mystery of *all that water.* As a child I had looked through a microscope at water from the streams and ponds of Minnesota. The water teemed with life. *Imagine all the life in the water of the Everglades,* I thought.

When Cindy suggested our next book be about the plan to restore the Everglades, I knew this would be an important and fascinating project. If we could involve some local children in the story of the Everglades and the efforts to restore it, we might help all children understand and appreciate what the Everglades means to the world.

At Avocado Elementary School in Homestead, Florida, we found Jacquelyn (Jackie) Stone and her fifth-grade class. Here was a teacher who was passionate about the Everglades and a class of charming, bright, questioning children who studied the Everglades as part of their regular curriculum.

Ms. Stone has been teaching the Everglades to children for more than twenty years. "We always do an Everglades unit. I show videos, we read books, and we do an experiment with sponges that shows the effects of water distribution. At the end we go on a field trip, and sometimes we have gone camping and slough slogging (wading through the Everglades)," she said.

Cindy and I were invited to explore the Everglades with the class, and Cindy visited the school for the experiment and other Everglades studies. There she saw a mural painted by some of the students. It represented the school's investment in the Everglades, both as an important subject to learn about and as a beautiful and mysterious inspiration for art.

"By teaching the Everglades, I am giving these children the responsibility, the legacy, to make sure the Everglades remains," said Ms. Stone. "I tell them I am leaving the Everglades to them."

Trish Marx, 2004

FURTHER READING

Doherty, Kieran. *Marjory Stoneman Douglas: Guardian of the 'Glades.* Twenty-First Century Books, 2002.

Douglas, Marjory Stoneman. *Alligator Crossing,* illustrated by Trudy H. Nicholson. Milkweed, reissued 2003.

Fazio, Wende. *Everglades National Park.* Children's Press, 1999.

George, Jean Craighead. *Everglades,* illustrated by Wendell Minor. HarperCollins, 1995.

Graf, Mike and David Szymanski. *Everglades National Park.* Bridgestone Books, 2003.

Stewart, Melissa. *Life in a Wetland,* photographed by Stephen K. Maka. Lerner, 2003.

Yolen, Jane. *Welcome to the River of Grass,* illustrated by Laura Regan. Putnam, 2001.

WEB SITES OF INTEREST

audubonofflorida.org

avocado.dadeschools.net

everglades.fiu.edu/index.htm

everglades.national-park.com

everglades.org

evergladesplan.org

florida-everglades.com

miamisci.org/ecolinks/everglades

nps.gov/ever/home.htm

GLOSSARY

adapt to adjust to different conditions, such as changes in the environment

alga (*pl.* **algae**) (AL-ga, *pl.* AL-jee) single-celled water plant that can make its own food; sometimes they form mats, as in periphyton

aquifer (AK-wa-fer) underground rock formation that contains or can contain water

blueprint detailed plan or outline for action

brackish slightly salty; a mix of freshwater and salty ocean water

dike bank of earth and stone used to control or hold back water

ecosystem (EK-oh-sis-tem *or* EE-koh-sis-tem) community of organisms and its environment functioning together

elevation height to which something is raised above sea level or the surface of the ground

endangered faced with the danger of becoming extinct and disappearing from Earth

food web diverse relationships of organisms linked through their food; often the smaller is eaten by the larger, which in turn is eaten by a still larger one

fungus (*pl.* **fungi**) (FUNG-ges, *pl.* FUN-jie) living organism without flowers, leaves, or chlorophyll which gets nourishment from dead or living organic matter

habitat place where a plant or an animal naturally lives and grows

hammock land rising out of a wetland, usually containing rich soil and hardwood trees

invertebrate (in-VER-te-brit) animal without a backbone

levee (LEV-ee) wall or bank built to prevent a river from overflowing

lichen (LIE-ken) plant consisting of a fungus and an alga growing together as one plant

marine found in or produced by the sea

marsh soft, wet, low-lying land, often with grasses and cattails growing in it; swamp

migrate to move from one region or climate to another, usually at certain set times

periphyton (pe-RIF-i-ton, *common usage:* per-ee-FIE-ton) loose association of microscopic organisms such as algae and fungi that live attached to underwater surfaces

phosphorus (FOS-fer-es) chemical element used in fertilizers; also a necessary component of plant and animal life

pollutant something that contaminates something else

pollution act or result of a pollutant contaminating something

porous (POUR-us) full of tiny holes through which water can pass

prairie (PRER-ee) relatively level grassland or meadow that may be covered with water

slough (slew) area of soft, muddy ground, such as a swamp or marsh

species (SPEE-shez) group of plants or animals with related characteristics; organisms of a species can breed only with each other

swamp wet, soft land often flooded at regular intervals; marsh

tannic acid (TAN-ik AS-id) chemical formed from bark and other vegetable matter

thermoregulate (thur-mo-REG-ye-late) to regulate body temperature; maintain a constant internal body temperature

wetland low land containing a great deal of moisture with wet, spongy soil